WHO'S HOLDING YOUR LADDER?

STUDY GUIDE

Copyright © 2025 by Sam Chand

Published by AVAIL

All rights reserved. No portion of this book may be reproduced, stored in a retrieval system, or transmitted in any form or by any means—electronic, mechanical, photocopy, recording, scanning, or other—except for brief quotations in critical reviews or articles, without prior written permission of the author.

For foreign and subsidiary rights, contact the author.

Cover design by: Sara Young
Cover photo by: Andrew van Tilborgh

ISBN: 978-1-964794-71-6   1 2 3 4 5 6 7 8 9 10

Printed in the United States of America

STUDY GUIDE

WHO'S HOLDING YOUR LADDER?

SAM CHAND

CONTENTS

CHAPTER 1. WHO'S HOLDING YOUR LADDER? 6

CHAPTER 2. WHAT KIND OF PERSON IS HOLDING YOUR LADDER? 12

CHAPTER 3. FIVE CORE QUALITIES OF LADDER HOLDERS 18

CHAPTER 4. HOW DO WE RECRUIT VOLUNTEERS? 24

CHAPTER 5. ARE WE MANAGING LADDERS? 30

CHAPTER 6. CAN WE TURN LADDER HOLDERS INTO LADDER CLIMBERS? 36

CHAPTER 7. ARE WE LOOKING UP THE LADDER? 42

CHAPTER 8. HOW DID JESUS CHOOSE LADDER HOLDERS? 48

CHAPTER 9. WHOSE LADDER ARE YOU HOLDING? 54

CHAPTER 1

WHO'S HOLDING YOUR LADDER?

Ultimately, the fulfillment of the vision depends on the people who support the ladder of the visionary leader.

READING TIME

As you read Chapter 1: "Who's Holding Your Ladder?" in *Who's Holding Your Ladder?* review, reflect on, and respond to the text by answering the following questions.

REFLECT AND TAKE ACTION:

Think about a time when you felt like you were climbing a "ladder" alone in leadership or ministry. What adjustments did you make to ensure you received the support you needed?

_____
_____
_____
_____
_____
_____

The ladder holder determines the height of the ladder climber. Who are the ladder holders in your life right now? Are they strengthening or limiting your ability to lead?

_____
_____
_____
_____
_____
_____

There are three ways leaders approach their work: doing everything themselves, hiring it out, or developing others. Which approach do you find yourself most often taking? What are the results of this approach?

_____
_____
_____
_____
_____
_____
_____
_____

Who in your organization have you trained, and who have you truly developed? What would it look like to prioritize development over training?

_____
_____
_____
_____
_____
_____
_____
_____

Who in your organization may be unable to hold the height of your ladder? Who are you holding onto that may have been able to hold your ladder in the past but isn't as capable now?

_____
_____

Have you ever placed someone in a leadership position based on skill rather than character? What was the result?

Leaders manage things, but they lead people. In what ways have you been managing people instead of leading them? How can you adjust your approach?

_____
_____
_____
_____
_____
_____
_____

If someone were to evaluate your leadership based on the strength of your ladder holders, what would they say? What steps can you take to build a stronger team of supporters?

_____
_____
_____
_____
_____
_____
_____

"Activity does not equal progress." Have you ever mistaken busyness for effectiveness? How can you ensure that your efforts are truly advancing your mission?

_____
_____
_____
_____
_____
_____
_____
_____

Consider the concept that ladder holders are often unseen. How does this challenge your view of leadership and influence? In what ways do you ensure their work does not go unnoticed?

_____
_____
_____
_____
_____
_____
_____
_____

CHAPTER 2

WHAT KIND OF PERSON IS HOLDING YOUR LADDER?

I want to make sure that my ladder holder understands what I'm trying to accomplish.

READING TIME

As you read Chapter 2: "What Kind of Person is Holding Your Ladder?" in *Who's Holding Your Ladder?* review, reflect on, and respond to the text by answering the following questions.

REFLECT AND TAKE ACTION:

Think about the people who currently support your leadership. Are they truly capable of holding your ladder at greater heights, or are they merely placeholders? How can you assess their commitment and ability?

_____
_____
_____
_____
_____
_____

Have you ever placed the wrong person in a key supporting role? What was the outcome, and what did you learn from that experience?

_____
_____
_____
_____
_____
_____

Are there people on your team who might not be the right ladder holders but could be better utilized in a different capacity? How can you reposition them for success?

_____
_____
_____
_____
_____
_____
_____

A leader cannot climb higher without the right ladder holders. Have you ever had to let go of someone who wasn't the right fit? How did that decision impact your leadership and organization?

_____
_____
_____
_____
_____
_____
_____

What are some warning signs that someone might not be a good ladder holder, even if they seem eager and willing? How can you recognize and address these early?

_____
_____
_____

Can you identify a ladder holder in your organization with the negative qualities described in this chapter? How have these negative qualities disrupted or hindered the height of your climb?

What specific qualities do you look for in those who support you? Are there any qualities you need to start prioritizing over others?

_____
_____
_____
_____
_____
_____
_____
_____

Consider a time when you felt unsupported or unstable in your leadership. What do you think was lacking in your team at that moment?

_____
_____
_____
_____
_____
_____
_____
_____

Are there any specific areas in your life or leadership where you need to strengthen your team to go further? How can you communicate that vision to your ladder holders?

_____
_____
_____
_____
_____
_____
_____

What is one specific change you can make in how you select, develop, or support those who hold your ladder?

_____
_____
_____
_____
_____
_____
_____

CHAPTER 3

FIVE CORE QUALITIES OF LADDER HOLDERS

We hire people for what they know; we fire them for who they are.

READING TIME

As you read Chapter 3: "Five Core Qualities of Ladder Holders" in *Who's Holding Your Ladder?* review, reflect on, and respond to the text by answering the following questions.

REFLECT AND TAKE ACTION:

If you were to ask your ladder holders what the vision of the church or organization is, would they all give the same answer? Why or why not?

_____
_____
_____
_____
_____
_____
_____
_____

Who on your team handles correction and criticism well? Who does not, and what actions need to be taken?

_____
_____
_____
_____
_____
_____
_____
_____

What are the indicators of an attentive team member? How do you spot inattentiveness, and what action steps do you take to confront it?

___

Have you ever experienced betrayal or abandonment in leadership? How did you respond, and what did it teach you about selecting the right ladder holders?

___

How well do you implement the "hire slowly and fire quickly" principle as the leader of your ministry or organization? Have you ever held onto a team member for too long? What held you back from making the necessary decision to fire?

___

Who in your organization allows manipulative people to exploit them? How does it impact their contribution to your vision and/or the mission of your organization as a whole?

Who are your followers, ministers, and leaders? Are they working in their giftings, or have they been placed in the wrong role?

___

In what ways are you training your ladder holders, and how do you know whether your approach is effective? What steps could you take to improve the way you train them?

___

In what ways do you fall into the "not enough time" trap when it comes to developing people?

_____
_____
_____
_____
_____
_____
_____
_____
_____

Whom from your organization would you call if you were marooned on an island? Whom wouldn't you call? What do your answers say about the ladder holders you have in place?

_____
_____
_____
_____
_____
_____
_____
_____
_____

CHAPTER 4

HOW DO WE RECRUIT VOLUNTEERS?

We need different ladder holders for different levels of ministry.

> ### READING TIME
>
> As you read Chapter 4: "How Do We Recruit Volunteers?" in *Who's Holding Your Ladder?* review, reflect on, and respond to the text by answering the following questions.

REFLECT AND TAKE ACTION:

Do you find yourself passively accepting volunteers or actively recruiting the right people? What challenges have you faced in shifting toward intentional recruitment?

_____
_____
_____
_____
_____
_____

Think about a time when you placed someone in a role they were not suited for. What was the outcome? How did it affect your team, and what would you do differently now?

_____
_____
_____
_____
_____
_____

How do you currently identify and assess the strengths of your team members? What adjustments might be needed in your approach?

_____
_____
_____
_____
_____
_____
_____

Are there individuals serving out of obligation rather than calling? How might you realign their roles to better suit their gifts and abilities?

_____
_____
_____
_____
_____
_____
_____

What do you think it means to view your volunteers as unpaid staff? How closely do your actions reflect that approach?

_____
_____
_____
_____

What systems do you currently have in place to ensure volunteers are properly trained and equipped? If none exist, what might an effective onboarding and training process look like for your ministry or organization?

How well do your volunteers understand the greater mission of your organization? How well do you understand your vision? What steps can you take to clarify and reinforce this vision?

_____
_____
_____
_____
_____
_____
_____

Leaders ask "what" and "why," while followers ask "how" and "when." Reflect on your leadership. Do you tend to focus more on logistical execution or casting vision? How might a shift in focus affect your team's effectiveness?

_____
_____
_____
_____
_____
_____
_____

How would you rate yourself as a communicator? What are you doing to prepare yourself to be a better communicator?

_____
_____
_____
_____
_____
_____
_____

How do generational differences impact volunteer engagement in your organization? What strategies can you implement to better connect and motivate a diverse group?

_____
_____
_____
_____
_____
_____
_____
_____

CHAPTER 5

ARE WE MANAGING LADDERS?

Leaders know where they want to reach. Managers know exactly where to position the ladder for the maximum benefit.

READING TIME

As you read Chapter 5: "Are We Managing Ladders?" in *Who's Holding Your Ladder?* review, reflect on, and respond to the text by answering the following questions.

REFLECT AND TAKE ACTION:

When you consider your leadership and management style, where do you naturally fit? Are you more of a leader or a manager?

_____
_____
_____
_____
_____
_____
_____

Leaders work from the future back to the present, while managers work from the past to the present. How does your perspective shape the way you plan and execute your responsibilities?

_____
_____
_____
_____
_____
_____
_____

In your ministry or organization, do you have the right balance of leaders and managers? How can you adjust your team's structure to create a more effective balance?

_____
_____
_____
_____
_____
_____

Think about a time when you initiated a new idea or project. Were there managers who resisted change? How did you handle their concerns, and how could you have navigated the tension between vision and structure more effectively?

_____
_____
_____
_____
_____
_____

Think about a time when you initiated a new idea or project. Were there managers who resisted change? How did you handle their concerns, and how could you have navigated the tension between vision and structure more effectively?

_____
_____

_____
_____
_____
_____
_____
_____

Reflect on a time when you had to take a major risk. How did it turn out? What did you learn about yourself and your approach to risk-taking?

_____
_____
_____
_____
_____
_____
_____
_____

Effective organizations evaluate leaders and managers differently. Are you currently measuring success in your leadership team appropriately? What changes might be needed?

_____
_____
_____
_____
_____
_____
_____
_____

How intentional are you about affirming the managers on your team? What can you do to better appreciate their contributions?

_____
_____
_____
_____
_____
_____
_____
_____

When implementing change, do you consider how people on your team will perceive loss versus gain? How can you improve communication to help team members embrace change?

_____
_____
_____
_____
_____
_____
_____
_____

Consider this statement: "If we wait until we're 100% sure, we're already too late." How does this challenge your current approach to decision-making? In what areas do you need to act more decisively?

_____
_____
_____
_____
_____
_____
_____
_____

CHAPTER 6

CAN WE TURN LADDER HOLDERS INTO LADDER CLIMBERS?

It's more difficult to unlearn than it is to learn.

READING TIME

As you read Chapter 6: "Can We Turn Ladder Holders into Ladder Climbers?" in *Who's Holding Your Ladder?* review, reflect on, and respond to the text by answering the following questions.

REFLECT AND TAKE ACTION:

Think about your own leadership journey. Did you start as a ladder holder before becoming a ladder climber? How did that process shape your leadership style?

_____
_____
_____
_____
_____
_____
_____

Who in your organization or ministry has the potential to climb but has not yet been given the opportunity? How can you develop and empower them?

_____
_____
_____
_____
_____
_____
_____

How intentional are you in guiding those around you to identify their passions, gifts, and calling? What specific steps can you take to improve this?

_____
_____
_____
_____
_____
_____
_____

Have you ever felt like you were experiencing a "near-life" moment? What held you back, and what helped you move forward? Have you ever observed this in someone else?

_____
_____
_____
_____
_____
_____
_____

Are you merely training people for tasks, or are you investing in their holistic growth as leaders? How can you shift toward a development mindset?

_____
_____
_____
_____

Unlearning is often harder than learning. What mindsets, habits, or leadership approaches do you need to unlearn to become more effective?

Think about someone who mentored you or helped you climb your leadership ladder. What did they do that made an impact? How can you replicate that for others?

_____
_____
_____
_____
_____
_____
_____

Leadership transitions can be painful, especially when long-time ladder holders are no longer fit for higher ladders. Have you ever had to make a difficult leadership shift? How did you navigate it, and what lessons did you learn?

_____
_____
_____
_____
_____
_____
_____

"Old leaders are rarely new leaders." How do you balance honoring those who have been faithful while also making room for fresh leadership?

_____
_____
_____
_____
_____
_____
_____
_____

What are you doing right now to multiply leaders within your organization? What is one practical step you can take this week to start developing someone new?

_____
_____
_____
_____
_____
_____
_____
_____

CHAPTER 7

ARE WE LOOKING UP THE LADDER?

The notion that you can make it at anything you want to do just isn't true.

READING TIME

As you read Chapter 7: "Are We Looking Up the Ladder?" in *Who's Holding Your Ladder?* review, reflect on, and respond to the text by answering the following questions.

REFLECT AND TAKE ACTION:

How often do you spend time with your team members to understand their passions and strengths? What questions can you start asking to help position people where they thrive?

_____
_____
_____
_____
_____
_____
_____

How do you currently assess team morale, and what strategies can you implement to improve job satisfaction and engagement?

_____
_____
_____
_____
_____
_____
_____

How can exceptional service and knowing your customers' or audiences' preferences be applied to your ministry or business? How well do you currently understand and serve your audience?

_____
_____
_____
_____
_____
_____
_____
_____

How clear are your organization's core identity and values? Do all team members understand and embody them?

_____
_____
_____
_____
_____
_____
_____
_____

In what ways do you struggle with impatience with the process of finding the right people to work the right jobs?

_____
_____
_____
_____

Does your leadership culture prioritize people over tasks? If not, what adjustments need to be made?

In your experience, have you seen a positive attitude make a greater impact than technical skill? How can you ensure your hiring and leadership development reflect this principle?

_____
_____
_____
_____
_____
_____
_____
_____

What kind of people is your organization attracting? How can you refine your team culture to draw in the right talent?

_____
_____
_____
_____
_____
_____
_____
_____

Who on your team is in the wrong seat on the bus? What steps can you take to transition them into a better fit without harming team morale?

_____
_____
_____
_____
_____
_____
_____
_____

Consider where your team members are placed within your organization. Are they happy there? How do you know? What will you do to find out?

_____
_____
_____
_____
_____
_____
_____
_____

CHAPTER 8

HOW DID JESUS CHOOSE LADDER HOLDERS?

People are recruited as ladder holders as a group, but they continue as individuals.

READING TIME

As you read Chapter 8: "How Did Jesus Choose Ladder Holders?" in Who's Holding Your Ladder? review, reflect on, and respond to the text by answering the following questions.

REFLECT AND TAKE ACTION:

Jesus didn't break up the partnership of Peter, James, and John. How do you view and manage existing relationships when bringing people into leadership? Have you ever overlooked the value of established partnerships?

_____
_____
_____
_____
_____
_____
_____

Think about a time when you failed to fully evaluate someone before placing them in a role. What were the consequences, and what did you learn?

_____
_____
_____
_____
_____
_____
_____

How do you assess and develop leadership potential in those around you?

_____
_____
_____
_____
_____
_____
_____

Are there people in your organization whose talents are underutilized? How can you help them align their abilities with their calling?

_____
_____
_____
_____
_____
_____
_____

Have you ever had team members questioning your leadership due to inaction? How can you improve responsiveness to organizational concerns?

_____
_____
_____

How do you create space for honest feedback from your team? Have you ever hesitated to make necessary leadership changes?

Do you treat your team primarily as a collective, or do you invest in their individual growth? How can you create a better balance?

_____
_____
_____
_____
_____
_____
_____

Have you ever found yourself delaying difficult decisions regarding personnel changes? What were the effects on your team, and what would you do differently next time?

_____
_____
_____
_____
_____
_____
_____

Think about a time when you made a necessary but difficult leadership decision. How did it impact morale and effectiveness?

_____
_____
_____
_____
_____
_____
_____
_____

In what ways does your leadership style reflect the example of Jesus? Where do you see gaps that need intentional improvement?

_____
_____
_____
_____
_____
_____
_____
_____

CHAPTER 9

WHOSE LADDER ARE YOU HOLDING?

God has called all of us to hold ladders for others.

READING TIME

As you read Chapter 9: "Whose Ladder Are You Holding?" in *Who's Holding Your Ladder?* review, reflect on, and respond to the text by answering the following questions.

REFLECT AND TAKE ACTION:

In what ways are you currently supporting someone else's leadership journey?

_____
_____
_____
_____
_____
_____

The chapter challenges leaders to ask, "What leader can I help?" rather than, "Who can help me?" Which question do you find yourself asking more? How does this shift in perspective challenge your current approach to leadership?

_____
_____
_____
_____
_____
_____

Are you modeling the kind of support and loyalty you want from your own ladder holders? Where do you need to grow?

_____
_____
_____
_____
_____
_____
_____

The law of reciprocity teaches that what we give will return to us. How have you seen this principle at work in your leadership? Where do you need to invest more intentionally in others?

_____
_____
_____
_____
_____
_____
_____

Leaders are often quick to seek support but slow to offer it. Have you ever hesitated to hold someone else's ladder? What held you back, and what was the outcome?

_____
_____
_____
_____

_____
_____
_____
_____

Who is climbing high because you stepped out of the way to support them? Are you making room for others to succeed? If not, what changes can you make?

_____
_____
_____
_____
_____
_____
_____
_____

Have you ever invested in the wrong ladder holder? How did you realize it, and what did you learn?

_____
_____
_____
_____
_____
_____
_____

How do you want to be remembered as a leader? What are you doing right now to ensure that your impact outlasts you?

_____
_____
_____
_____
_____
_____
_____

Are you trying to do too much on your own? How can you embrace the support of a team?

_____
_____
_____
_____
_____
_____
_____

What immediate steps can you take to be a better ladder holder for someone this week? Identify one person you can support, encourage, or invest in and make a plan to take action.

_____
_____
_____
_____
_____
_____
_____

www.ingramcontent.com/pod-product-compliance
Lightning Source LLC
Chambersburg PA
CBHW062123080426
42734CB00012B/2968